Vicky's Journey

From East to West

Vicky Meyer

Onwards and Upwards Publishers

3 Radfords Turf
Cranbrook
Exeter
EX5 7DX
United Kingdom

www.onwardsandupwards.org

This first edition published in the United Kingdom by Onwards and Upwards Publishers (2017).

ISBN: 978-1-78815-635-6
Typeface: Sabon LT
Graphic design: LM Graphic Design

Printed in the United Kingdom.

Endorsements

Here is an engaging story of a life formed in hardship and lived with fortitude, facing losses accompanying disability as well as those from a succession of family tragedies. I came to know Vicky and husband Walter when in St Albans, and my abiding memories are of the strength of personality and Christian maturity they contributed to the fellowship of the church there, and of Vicky's curious walking sticks! Now, years later, we are again in touch as with her sight loss Vicky has turned to Torch Trust for accessible Christian reading.

Though brought up by Christian parents it was only after living independently that Vicky found faith for herself, a faith in Jesus that has clearly been the foundation of her security and stability ever since. There's a line from a familiar Christian song that captures for me the testimony of Vicky's well-lived life: "Father, I place into your hands the things that I've been through."

Dr Gordon Temple
CEO, Torch Trust

This is the story of a remarkable life journey, its difficulties and joys. It is told with a lightness of touch that belies the impact on Vicky of its hardship and pain, as a child interned by the Japanese during the Second World War, and in the griefs of family life.

We see how her courage and resilience in the face of adversity is firmly rooted in her faith and her hope in God. I found this book a fascinating and inspiring read.

Sarah Frettingham
Psychotherapist and churchwarden

Ann, later to be known as Vicky, and I were born in the same year and our families, six Chalkleys and five Houghtons, lived next door to each other on the compound of the Chefoo School. Her parents and mine were CIM missionaries and members of the school staff.

Like Ann, I was interned under the Japanese in north China and came to England in 1945 after the war. When we met again, in 1950, Ann had become a Christian and was living in Mussel Hill.

Years later, when I was a missionary on home leave, she invited me to speak at a women's meeting of the Brethren Assembly to which she and her husband belonged. I remember meeting Walter then and seeing some of the walking sticks he had collected.

Our paths have differed widely. This is a good time to look back, as Ann does, and reflect on her experiences of joy and sorrow, and to look forward with Christian hope.

Felicity Bentley-Taylor
Former missionary in Chile and Bolivia

From China to Thixendale (a remote village in Yorkshire). That's quite a journey, and so is Vicky Meyer's autobiography.

When I first met Vicky, it was soon obvious she'd led a very interesting life. Her fascinating walking sticks are works of art every one! But, of course, it's Vicky's journey, so amazing and full of trepidation, especially during her early years in a Japanese internment camp during WWII, that makes this such a great story. I hope you enjoy it as much as I have.

M. Christina Butler
Children's author

Vicky gives us a fascinating and absorbing first-hand account of living as a child in Japanese-occupied China and the complete contrast of growing into adulthood in post war London. She shares the joys and the sorrows, the blessings and the heartbreak of being a parent and grandparent.

This autobiography is a moving illustration of the hymn Vicky heard sung in the POW camp at the funeral of Eric Liddell, the *Chariots of Fire* missionary.

Be still, my soul, the Lord is on thy side
Bear patiently the cross of grief and pain
Leave to thy God to order and provide
In every change he faithful will remain.

Bishop David James

Acknowledgements

Many times over the years, my family and friends have asked me to tell them about my past, particularly my childhood. Often, when I have recounted incidents, I have been told that I should make a written recording of the stories. I had never seriously considered this task until I came to live in Yorkshire and was greatly encouraged by a new friend, David, to write this book with his help. His input and hard work is enormously appreciated.

With my eyesight failing, the next steps of finding and working with the publisher, Onwards and Upwards, fell on my daughter, Cherith, who spent hours and hours typing and emailing, for which I am very grateful. Without her, this book would never have been published. I am also grateful to Cherith's husband, Andy, for his patience and support.

My thanks go to those who have read and endorsed the book and my hope is that it will provide blessing and encouragement to all who read it.

Dedicated to everyone who
has been part of my
journey.

Vicky's Journey

Contents

Vicky's Journey

Foreword by Cherith Judson

WHEN OUR FAMILY WAS YOUNG, Mother was the one we children went to for comfort. Her life had not been short on suffering and she knew how to offer solace, whatever situation had driven us into her arms.

These are the memoirs she has chosen to share.

In the book, as in the telling of her story during our childhood, Mother is matter-of-fact, succinct and to the point. In between the lines, as in the pauses as we listened, is an unspoken depth – the hidden pain. Yet I seldom hear her complain; rather, she seeks out cheer wherever it may be found.

Mother is grateful for the good whilst accepting of the bad, the ugly. Her story, for that reason, offers hope in the darkest of places even though there are sometimes no answers to the question, "Why?"

It is Mother's unswerving faith that has kept her going, although it has not always been so. As a child, she was angered by a God who allowed her world to fall apart; as a teenager, she began to know that same God in another way: as fellow sufferer, a recipient of cruelty, abandoned and distraught.

Mother's commitment to God has helped her to accept the past and has carried her through to the present day. Sharing her story has taken courage – her desire and prayer is that, in the reading of her journey, others will also take courage and, where answers are scarce and hope is difficult to come by, they might also find solace.

Vicky's Journey

CHAPTER ONE

The Early Years in China

I WAS NOT ACTUALLY BORN in China, yet much of my early life centres on that unique and enthralling country at a specific time in its history. I was there because my parents, Harold and Lillian Chalkley, were missionaries, although at the time of my birth they were back in the United Kingdom on furlough. I actually saw the first light of day, therefore, in the Maple Nursing Home, situated in the Hertfordshire town of Hitchin. This was on 8 June 1933.

Since Hitchin was my father's place of birth and where he had his family roots, it was a logical place for me to be born and as good a place as any other. My father's grandfather (my great grandfather) had, in actual fact, started the Hitchin Fire Brigade, back in the days when the tender was horse-drawn. My father would often recall having to walk, as a young lad, in front of the first motor car that came to the town, waving a red flag to warn pedestrians that the new vehicle was coming their way.

My mother and father had met as childhood friends when my mother was six and my father was seven. My mother was the daughter of a minister in Baldock in Hertfordshire; my father was a member of a congregational church in Hitchin – and they had grown up together.

My parents often recalled, quite vividly, a church outing when they went to Dunstable Downs. They remembered sitting on the grass and listening to James Hudson Taylor – the guest speaker – who talked about China and the work that he and others were doing there.

That was the first time (when they were teenagers) that my mother and father became interested in China and the China Inland Mission (CIM). Little did they know at the time that they would eventually become missionaries to China themselves – nor that they would eventually get married in a Chinese town called Chefoo.

Lillian and Harold Chalkley.

James Hudson Taylor was a British Christian missionary who spent fifty-one years in China, having founded the China Inland Mission. There had been Christian influences in the coastal towns of China, particularly Shanghai, and also in Hong Kong (there was actually a cathedral in Hong Kong very early on) but no one had taken the Christian message into other parts of the country. James Hudson Taylor had been there, had seen the situation and felt called to take the message to those living inland; hence the title 'China Inland Mission'. It is still in existence, although it is now called the 'Overseas Missionary Fellowship' (OMF International) because, officially, missionaries are no longer allowed to enter China.

James was born in Barnsley, South Yorkshire, on 21 May 1832, the son of a pharmacist and Methodist lay preacher, James Taylor, and his wife, Amelia Hudson. He professed faith in Christ at the age of seventeen and in December 1849, he committed himself to going to China as a missionary.

In 1851, Hudson Taylor moved to a poor neighbourhood in Kingston upon Hull where he became a medical assistant and began preparing himself for a life of faith and service. He devoted himself to the poor and began to exercise his faith in believing that God would provide for his needs. It was here that Hudson Taylor began to distribute gospel tracts and practised open-air preaching among the poor.

James Hudson Taylor was baptised by a member of the Plymouth Brethren in the Hull Brethren Assembly in 1852 and, in the same year, he began studying medicine (as preparation for working in China) at the Royal London Hospital in Whitechapel, London.

Taylor was best known for his sensitivity to Chinese culture as well as his zeal for evangelism. He chose to wear native Chinese clothing even though, at that particular time, this was rare among missionaries.

Under Taylor's leadership, the CIM was notably non-denominational and accepted members from all Protestant groups. CIM also included individuals from the working classes, as well as single women.

Harold in his Ambulance Brigade uniform
during the First World War.

My mother went to a Bible school for training when the First World War broke out, whilst my father, who was a conscientious objector, joined the St John's Ambulance Brigade. He was sent out to France and worked on a train that used to bring back the injured soldiers from the battlefields to the hospital.

As soon as the war was over, my mother was able to travel to China – in those days it was a very long journey and would take nearly six weeks to travel from England to Shanghai – and she went on her own. After six weeks in Shanghai, she was sent inland to work. My father was committed to his employment with the St John's Ambulance Brigade for some time and didn't manage to get out to China until 1920.

The Mission sent my father and mother to Chefoo to work in the school set up for missionaries' children. My father was a language teacher and my mother worked as a House Mother to all the younger girls and boys.

There was a very strict rule in those days that any missionaries belonging to the China Inland Mission who wanted to get married in China must have been in the country for at least two years. Therefore, it was not until 1922 that my parents were able to get married and, because they had no parents of their own out there to arrange a wedding, an older missionary couple, Arthur and Lela Taylor, arranged their wedding for them.

The Taylors had a daughter called Mary, who became my parents' bridesmaid. Years later, Mary returned to China as a missionary herself and she, too, wanted to get married; as her parents weren't there, my own parents acted *in loco parentis,* and I was her bridesmaid at about six years of age. To this day, I still have the dress that I wore, in my wardrobe here in Yorkshire.

My own particular story continues with a very happy early childhood in Chefoo (now known as Yantai) in

Northern China. Within a few weeks of my birth, my parents had returned there, arriving back with the new addition to their family. Although I was officially named Grace Ann Chalkley, my immediate family members called me Ann (and still do, to this day). The nickname Vicky was introduced when I was a teenager and has somehow managed to stick!

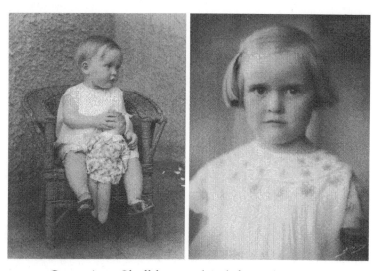

Grace Ann Chalkley aged 2 (left) and 4 (right).

In Chefoo, there was a large missionary school which had a very good reputation and was extremely popular with all sorts of people. It had been set up by James Hudson Taylor as part of his work in establishing the China Inland Mission, and the school had originally provided an education for the children of those missionaries with whom he worked. The school, however, acquired such a high status in the field of education that many other people who were not missionaries soon began to send their children there.

The Chalkley family in Chefoo.
Left to right: Harold, Mary & Betty (the twins),
Grace Ann, Lillian and Donovan.

The Chefoo Missionary School was established in 1881. It began life adjacent to a sanatorium for sick missionaries, but soon grew larger than the hospital itself. Between 1881 and 1886, the number of pupils grew to over one hundred, resident in three departments – the boys', girls' and preparatory school. In 1886, the boys' and girls' schools were separated and enlargements were made to the girls' school.

The Chefoo Missionary School.

The name of the school was originally the Protestant Collegiate School but by 1908 the name 'China Inland Mission School' was generally used. By 1947, the name 'Chefoo School' had been adopted, which referred to the style of education rather than the actual place. It was a Christian boarding school.

Members of staff at Chefoo School were required to be full members of the China Inland Mission. The curriculum was based on the British system, heavily weighted in favour of classical courses designed to prepare students for entrance to British universities including Oxford and Cambridge. There was also an emphasis on religious education. The principal at Chefoo School led prayers daily, and there were two church services held each Sunday.

There were four school terms beginning in February, April, August and October. The school also had a strong reputation for sports, such as football and rowing. Headmasters at Chefoo School included Pat Bruce (1930-1945) and Stanley Houghton (1947-1950).

Under Pat Bruce, the various innovations at Chefoo School included the creation of the Chefoo Orchestra in 1930; the introduction of co-education in 1934; the teaching of Chinese studies; and the beginning of a Girl Guides company. In 1936, Chefoo School also adopted the Chinese dolphin as its crest.

The Chefoo School adopted the Chinese dolphin as its crest.

Following the war and the occupation of North China by Communist forces, the school was temporarily located at the China Inland Mission headquarters in Shanghai. In 1951, the China Inland Mission decided to withdraw completely from China, so staff and students of Chefoo School moved to Hong Kong. Sadly, Chefoo School in China ceased to exist.

Chefoo is in the Shantung Province of Northern China, right up near the Korean borders. It was a pretty town as well as being a seaside port that had many ships coming and leaving, even though the port, as I remember, had extremes of temperature – almost a microclimate of its own. In the winter months, the sea would often freeze over and one time an American ship became frozen in the harbour and was unable to leave for weeks. During that period, the crew on board the stranded vessel decided to host a party for all the local schoolchildren; this was truly a special occasion in which we enjoyed the delights of jelly and ice-cream, musical chairs and 'pin the tail on the donkey' to name but a few. When the day arrived, I was able to walk across the frozen harbour in order to board the ship. It has always been a personal amusement for me that I can honestly say I have walked on water!

Another of my earliest memories was going for a picnic. Although we had many happy hours on the beach in Chefoo (and, being close to the sea, I recall the school having a number of rowing boats as well as teams of rowers), there were also the hills that rose fairly sharply behind the compound where we all lived. My family, which consisted of twin sisters and a brother (who were older than me), as well as my mother and father, took a picnic up into the hills. This was probably in about 1937/38.

From around 1937 onwards, the Japanese, whose emperor had decided that he wanted to have world domination, had invaded Northern China; there were Japanese soldiers all over the place. We were very used to seeing them and, generally speaking, they were amicable, friendly, obviously liked children and were quite easy to get on with.

At the time when we took the picnic up into the hills, there was a Japanese sentry box a little way farther up from where we were picnicking. I was perhaps five years old at the time, or maybe a little younger, and I had decided that I would go and have a look at the soldier who was sitting in this box. So, I climbed up and looked inside. The Japanese guard appeared to be asleep – which I thought was a bit odd – so I poked him, but he didn't wake up.

I then went back to my family and told my father that the Japanese guard was asleep. My father knew that this seemed a bit odd, so he went to the sentry box (and I went back with him) and he realised the chap was not asleep but that he was actually dead. The soldier had a bullet hole right through his heart!

That was the first time, I think, that I saw a dead body (unfortunately, not the last). Needless to say, it was quite a shock to discover that the guard was, in fact, dead – and it definitely ruined that picnic day.

I have other early memories, too, especially of going for walks with my mother, probably when I was pre-school age; it was something she used to do after breakfast every morning. My mother would walk to the city gates where there was a small building – it was like a miniature pagoda and it had a very special purpose. This small building was used by those mothers who had given birth to girls that they didn't want; they would take the babies and place them inside it.

A Chinese pagoda.

In the Chinese culture, and especially at that time (in the 1930s) when there wasn't any contraception, there were huge families and the children that were appreciated, of course, were the boys. Traditional Chinese family values featured very different and clear-cut roles and rights for men and women. In the traditional Chinese family, the man was responsible for maintaining, providing for and protecting his family. At the same time, he was given all the decision-making power when it came to his wife, his children (until they were married) and other family members. On the other hand, women usually stayed at home to take care of the house, the children and the rest of the extended family.

Chinese culture valued patrilineal descent, whereby a child's lineage was calculated from the male side of the family only. Men were the only ones who could inherit family land or acquire other types of inheritance. This perceived and enforced inferiority of women greatly influenced the way in which children were looked at – many baby girls were killed or abandoned at birth. So quite a lot of girls would be taken and placed in these pagodas. My mother used to go every day to see if there was a baby there and, if there was, she would rescue it and take it to an orphanage in the town which was run by Catholic nuns.

A particularly special early memory is that one of the visitors who used to arrive in Chefoo at that time was a lady called Gladys Aylward. She is quite well known because of the film that was made of her life called 'The Inn of the Sixth Happiness'[1].

Gladys May Aylward was a British evangelical Christian missionary who went to China on her own. She had been a domestic worker (housemaid) but always had a calling to go overseas as a missionary. However, since she was not educated, no missionary society would send her. Gladys had therefore saved up her own money, which enabled her to come across on the trans-Siberian railway from Europe, right over to China where she was working inland.

For a time, Gladys served as an assistant to the Chinese government and travelled around the countryside as a 'foot inspector' (a position that my mother also held). Her task was to enforce the new law against foot-binding young Chinese girls. She proved to be extremely successful, even where there had been much resistance including, on occasions, violence towards the inspectors. In 1936, Gladys Aylward became a Chinese citizen and was highly respected

---

[1] Twentieth Century Fox, 1958

among the people, having taken in orphans as well as adopting several herself; having intervened during a volatile prison riot and supported prison reform; as well as risking her life many times to help those in need.

When the region was invaded by Japanese forces, Gladys led over a hundred orphans to safety, travelling over the mountains, despite being wounded herself. She not only led them to safety, but personally cared for them and led many of them to Christ.

Gladys never married, but spent her entire life devoting herself to Christ and working among the people of China. Eventually, in 1948, Gladys came back to Britain; then, after ten years, she requested a return to China but was denied re-entry by the Communist government. However, Gladys decided to go to Taiwan, where she founded the Gladys Aylward Orphanage, and she worked there until her death in 1970.

During her time in China, Gladys used to come down to Chefoo for relaxation, for a holiday and for a rest. The missionaries who were there would also 'employ' her (in order to help her) and paid her for looking after their children and for helping in the school.

After all this, the next very significant thing that I remember was hearing that the Japanese, in their quest for world domination, had attacked Pearl Harbour and involved America in the war. At that point, all the foreigners in China were considered enemies and it was quite frightening to have the Japanese now not so friendly.

One day Japanese soldiers came and stuck a notice on the front of our house, which informed us that the house was now the property of the Japanese emperor. The soldiers went through all the houses on the compound where we lived, as well as all the school rooms, and they confiscated every radio that was there (there were no televisions in those days) – these had been our only contact with the outside world, and they all disappeared. So, we were left quite in the dark as to what was going on.

Chapter Two

Japanese Imprisonment

WE WERE TOLD THAT WE could no longer leave the actual compound where the school was. We were not allowed to wander down to the beach or up into the hills; we were confined to the compound. Nevertheless (and because the campus was fairly spacious with school buildings, a playground and cricket pitch), it seemed that for a few weeks, or maybe a few months, it was life as usual, more or less – except for the knowledge, of course, that we were now enemies of the Japanese.

Then came the day in 1942 (I was nine years old) when the Japanese commander came to the school and we were informed that all of those present would be taken off to the concentration camp. He didn't say when and he didn't say where; we just knew we were going to be interned. He instructed us that all we could take was one piece of luggage each – he didn't specify the size, but it was just one piece of luggage per person.

I remember my mother giving me a suitcase and telling me to put good, decent, warm clothing in it – the winters were very cold there and the summers were very hot. It was the winters that my mother was worried about.

I, however, had other ideas. I had a pet rabbit called Peter, and Peter was part of our family. So, I decided to put holes in the bottom of my suitcase and put my rabbit in it instead of my clothes. I would then be able to take Peter with me into the camp.

This was not appreciated very much by my mother when she discovered my secret plan, so Peter was left behind and the suitcase filled with some warm clothes and shoes. Leaving Peter behind was such a great disappointment, as was the fact that my doll, a Shirley Temple doll, had also to be abandoned.

The day soon came when the Japanese suddenly arrived with many trucks and a large number of soldiers. We were told to put all of our baggage onto the trucks and that we would be taken to the concentration camp. We were expected to line up and to walk. We didn't know if we were heading down towards the harbour and being put onto a ship, or whether we were to walk across to the other side of Chefoo.

I do remember the extreme disappointment of two or three of the staff members because they had been so sure that the Lord would look after us and not allow anyone to be interned. It was a great test of their faith, therefore, as well as the faith of the children, for us to be put into the camps.

As it turned out, we were made to walk across the town, to the other side of Chefoo, where there was a road called

Temple Hill. There were a lot of buildings that had been put up by oil companies which had once been busy in the local vicinity. Many of these buildings were, in fact, very nice and somewhat large houses. We were told that we were to be accommodated in two of these houses.

The Japanese split us into two groups – they put all the boys into one group and all the girls into another, each with various staff members. There were ninety-six children in the school at the time, all without their parents. The invasion of Pearl Harbour had taken place on 8 December (the previous year), which was term time and the children were still at school. Had the invasion occurred a week later, the school would have broken up for the school holidays and the children would have been dispersed all over China and back to their parents. Many of the children started at the school from the tender age of six, so there was an enormous group of young children there, as well as all the different age groups up to sixth-form level.

When we were eventually told to march out of the compound, the Japanese lined the children up and as we went out of the gates of the compound, someone began to sing the words of a chorus that we all knew:

> *God is still on the throne,*
> *and he will remember his own;*
> *Though trials may press us*
> *and burdens distress us,*
> *He never will leave us alone.*
> *God is still on the throne;*
> *and he will remember his own;*

His promise is true,
  He will not forget you.
God is still on the throne.

So, we walked out singing. The Chinese, who had always been our friends, were distraught to see us go and there were many tears shed.

Eventually we arrived on Temple Hill (there were over fifty of us in the girls' camp) and we discovered that our sleeping arrangements were in the loft of a particularly large house. The mattresses were laid out all over the floor, all very close to each other, so if you wanted to get up in the night, you invariably had to step over bodies.

The staff quarters were equally cramped. My mother and father had to share a very small room with another couple, but they managed to get a curtain down the middle of the room so that each couple had one half as their bedroom.

Life at Temple Hill was extremely odd. My father was a teacher – he was a language teacher who taught French, Latin and Greek. There were also other members of the teaching staff interned at the camp, so they tried to give us lessons. Sometimes these were taken outdoors (if the weather was warm enough) and sometimes they were taken while we were sitting on the mattresses in the loft. The staff even tried to keep the Girl Guides and the Brownies going.

I enrolled in the Brownies and was very proud of the brown uniform. However, I cannot remember much about what I did to earn my badges; it was all very confined, everyone seemed to be on top of each other and, to make matters worse, we didn't know how long we were going to

31

be there. As it turned out, we stayed in Temple Hill for several months.

Then, in September 1943, the Japanese commandant informed us that we were going to be transferred to a much larger internment camp in inland China. We were not told where it was, but we were informed that we all had to be packed up with our one piece of luggage ready to go on a certain date.

CHAPTER THREE

Weihsien Camp

THE DAY DULY ARRIVED when we left Temple Hill, walking down through the city of Chefoo and down to the harbour. We boarded a Japanese troop ship, which left an awful lot to be desired, and we were taken on a three-day journey down the coast of China to the port of Tsingtao. On our arrival, we were offloaded from the boat and transferred onto trucks; it was at this point we were informed that we were being taken to a camp at Weihsien.

We arrived at Weihsien and discovered it was extremely different to the camp at Temple Hill. It was much larger, almost like a village, and had been built by the Presbyterian missionaries as a school and a seminary where they educated the Chinese and also prepared Chinese pastors for ministry. There were rows upon rows of single-room huts where previously the students had stayed, and there were one or two other buildings, including a church and a hospital. There was also a large lecture hall and a playing field.

We soon discovered that the camp was spread around one street, which we all called 'Main Street', and as we were unloaded from the trucks, we were told to march up this street.

To our surprise, we then realised that the camp was already occupied and, with the addition of those from Chefoo, would house about 1,600; all the nationalities that you could imagine were there. These internees had, of course, already heard that we were arriving, so they had lined the main street (and every other available viewpoint) to see who we were. They were astonished to see that we were, in fact, ninety children with various members of staff.

On the first night in this new camp, we were not taken to the rows of small houses but to a much bigger building, where we were shown into a room that was completely bare. This was where we were to spend the night. We didn't know at the time if this was where we were going to stay permanently, but I do remember that the building had a concrete floor and we were told to settle down. I wondered what we were going to sleep on.

My father had been wearing a raincoat, so he put it on the floor and told me to lie down on it and go to sleep. Being a concrete floor, it was most uncomfortable, especially lying on just a raincoat. A lady came in who was one of the internees already in the camp; she was an American missionary. She saw the predicament and told my father to keep me awake while she went away and came back with a single bed eiderdown. That, to me, was absolute heaven! My father wrapped me in the eiderdown, even though I still lay on his raincoat. Now I was warm and comfortable.

Life in the camp had been organised already by the people who were there before us. There were three kitchens installed, which split the camp into three different feeding places. We were assigned to kitchen number 1 and we used to go there for such food as there was. They served what they called 'breakfast', which was a type of gruel, meant to be porridge, but no sugar, no milk and very lumpy. This was served every morning. Later in the day – about five o'clock in the evening – we were served our main meal, which was meant to be sufficient for everybody.

One morning, after breakfast, I was coming out of the place where we were eating. There had been a delivery of the ingredients for the evening meal, which was on a table outside the kitchen. There was what appeared to be a large lump of meat, but I thought it looked really strange; it was black and, although I wasn't very old, I had never seen black meat before. So, I went over and touched it. I immediately discovered that it was a huge flank of horse meat and was covered with flies. As I touched the meat, they all flew up; it was quite disgusting! However, the horse meat was cooked – it was boiled and thrashed and whatever else they did to it – and all the time we were in that camp, we never saw anything but horse meat.

I suppose it is because of this experience (and, perhaps, because of the Eastern upbringing that I had) that I really don't understand why people nowadays get so worked up about, or are disapproving of, horse meat when we are quite happy to eat a cow, a sheep or a pig. It doesn't seem very logical to me not to eat a horse too.

Everyone over the age of ten had to work. When my turn came, my first job was helping to clean the latrines, which were trenches with stepping stones either side for your feet. It was absolutely disgusting!

Far worse, from the internees' point of view, was the issue of boredom. Since no news was available, various rumours would be spread around the camp – rumours about all sorts of things, but it was all made up. There was, however, a crystal radio set in the camp, which was dismantled and the various components kept by different internees. Every now and then, they would get together and assemble it so we could listen to the BBC world news. That was passed round the camp and became the only real contact we had with the outside world.

On one occasion, after we had settled down to daily life in the camp, I said to my father, "Well, we can't tithe now because we've got no money." I had, obviously, been brought up in a Christian home and had been instructed from the Bible about tithing. The Japanese had taken everything – they had taken our home, all of the money, the bank accounts were closed – so, as a rather cheeky nine- or ten-year-old, I pressed him, "We can't tithe, can we?" My father gave me a rather strange look and said, "I'll think about that, dear, and come back to you."

He came back to me later the same day and said that he had thought about what I had asked. He had decided that it *was* possible to tithe but because all we had now was time, it needed to be done differently. He said that since we had twelve hours of each day when we were allowed to move around the camp, we were going to tithe that; we would make sure that at least one hour and twelve minutes of each day was spent helping somebody else or doing something for the Lord. I later came to quite respect him for that decision.

Someone else that I came to respect at this time, and who was a big personality in the camp, was a man called Eric Liddell. He is someone who has since become extremely well-known.

Eric first came into the public arena when he was taking part in the 1924 Olympics in Paris. His race, the hundred metres, was scheduled to be run on a Sunday but being a Christian, Eric refused to run on what he considered a day of rest. This put the organisers in a bit of a tizzy so, in the end, they decided to put him into the four hundred metres, a race he had never competed in but one which was run on a Tuesday. Eric ran that race and he won it. His story has been made into a film, *Chariots of Fire,* which has been shown all over the world.

When war broke out, Eric was in China as a missionary with his wife and two little daughters. His wife was Canadian and there was a repatriation system whereby a few people were allowed to leave, even after Pearl Harbour. Eric's wife was pregnant so he decided that his wife and his two little girls should get on the repatriation list and go back to Canada where she had family. It was agreed that Eric would follow as soon as he could afterwards. So, his wife and daughters left and Eric stayed. Unfortunately, Eric never did manage to get repatriated and he spent the rest of his life in that camp.

It was quite interesting for everybody in the camp to note the change in one of Eric's beliefs: his attitude to Sunday sports. In the camp, everybody over the age of ten had to work, and had to work six days a week. Sunday was the only day when there was any relaxation and the day when we didn't have to work. Eric Liddell, who was such a keen sportsman, knew that all the children in the camp needed some sort of sporting activity, so he arranged football matches, races, athletics – all sorts of things that we could do on a Sunday. I felt that spoke volumes of the man; that he adapted to the changed circumstances in order to use his own God-given abilities to help others in the camp.

Job application form, Weihsien Camp.

Meanwhile, the lack of food in the camp was obvious; but worse was the lack of water. Water was very restricted and we all came to realise that thirst could be much worse than hunger. Water was rationed and we were each allocated a certain amount at the start of the day.

There were quite a few medics in the camp (doctors and nurses who had been working in China) and they were concerned that all the children in the camp were not getting anything like the diet that they should have. They could see a lot of problems coming, and one of the things that was very lacking was calcium for strong bones and growth. The doctors and nurses got their heads together and they decided that they would ask those who did the cooking to keep all the eggshells that they used.

Eggshells have a lot of calcium in them so the eggshells were ground up as much as they could be, in a sort of pestle and mortar, and we were expected to take a spoonful of ground-up eggshell every morning to make up for the lack of calcium. I don't know if you have ever tried to swallow eggshell but it is not a pleasant experience. If we had had lots of water to swill it down, it probably would have been easier; then we could have got rid of it, rather than it sticking in our throats. With the lack of water, however, we had to try to get this teaspoonful of eggshell down with one gulp. It was absolute agony; we hated it.

The medics told us that we ought to be grateful that there were *any* eggs. It was understood later that a lot of the eggs had come into the camp on what was known as the 'black market'. This was largely due to the monks who were in the camp. They were not a silent order of monks, but they wore long brown tunics and one of them had a particular spot where he used to go and pray; this was by the external wall of the camp which had barbed wire on top of it. He used to sit there and spread his robes out and have his Bible in front of him.

Unbeknown to many of us, this monk had managed to contact those Chinese who came into the camp to deliver things. They had dug a hole under the wall and used to roll eggs through, which he then gathered up under his tunic. Although it was, no doubt, very good of him to do this, we children hated him – it was because of him that there was never any lack of eggshell.

Eric Liddell, on the other hand, was very popular in the camp. He was great fun; he wore ridiculous shirts that were very bright – red and white and turquoise – and he always made us laugh. It was very sad when we realised that he wasn't very well. He was diagnosed with a brain tumour.

Eric was put into the hospital wing, which was operating with very few medicines. The Salvation Army boys who came into the camp had been allowed to bring their brass instruments with them and they used to come and play outside the hospital block every Sunday. On the last Sunday he was alive, Eric sent a message out to the brass band requesting that they would, please, play the hymn *Be Still My Soul, the Lord is On Thy Side* to the tune *Finlandia*. We all heard it and knew that it was Eric's request. By the time the band came to play again, Eric had passed away.

My parents, my sisters and I had a room in the hospital block (my brother Donovan being housed in the boys' dormitory) and Eric Liddell had been to our room the day before he died. I remember that my mother made him a cup of tea before he went back to his bed in the hospital.

Eric's funeral was held in the church on the compound and it was absolutely full – there were hundreds of people. I think the whole camp must have turned out as people were also standing round the church and on the playing field. He was buried just outside the walls of the camp. Only a few people were allowed to go with the coffin to where Eric was buried; another little service was held at the graveside.

That wasn't the only funeral that we saw; there were many people who didn't make it through those years in the concentration camp. One particular incident was very close to home. When we were called out on roll-call (which we had to do every day), we stood in lines on a playing field and waited for the Japanese soldiers to come along. They would count us and make sure that everyone was there. We often had to wait a long time, sometimes in the cold and sometimes in the burning heat. The children, obviously, became restless. On one occasion, my brother was standing with his friend, Brian Thompson, and some other lads, when they discovered a wire – an electric wire – that ran across the playground to one of the sentry boxes in a corner of the camp. This wire hung down low and the boys, bored with waiting for the soldiers to arrive, decided that they would each try to reach it. They jumped up to catch hold of this wire and Brian Thompson, who was the tallest, managed to grab it. It proved to be a live wire and Brian pulled it down. He received a tremendous electric shock whilst, at the same time, the wire cut across the neck of my brother (he had that scar across his neck all of his life). Unfortunately, Brian died. Brian's mother, brother and sister were also in the camp and I think they were possibly the only ones who were allowed to go outside the camp for his burial. Brian's death and funeral were such a shock that I don't think we ever misbehaved during another roll call ever again. We just stood there, patiently waiting for the Japanese to count us.

There are many places near that camp that are precious to various families and the Chinese are very proud of the fact that Eric Liddell died there. What had been the camp is now a school and the Chinese have raised a plaque to Eric Liddell outside the school grounds. Eric's two elder daughters went to China for the unveiling of the plaque, so it is nice to know that he is remembered there as well as in other places.

During the four years of the war, the Red Cross were very active in sending parcels – "comfort parcels" – to internees, all of whom were prisoners of war. We learned, after the war, that the prisoners in Weihsien had, during the course of the war, been sent parcels on forty-four different occasions. These had mainly come from the American Red Cross – perhaps a tenth from the British Red Cross.

I often ask people to guess how many of those forty-four parcel deliveries we ever received, and the guesses are quite interesting. In actual fact, of those forty-four we only ever received one! That one parcel arrived towards the end of the war, when the Japanese knew they were beaten – I think they gave us the parcels to try to make reparations.

I had personally never seen anything like the contents of those parcels. The one I received had chewing gum (which I had never heard of) and all sorts of other things, including something that I really enjoy to this day: a tin of Spam! I had never tasted anything like it before and to me it was heavenly. I also had a tin of Del Monte peaches, which were so lovely and sweet and juicy.

The other forty-three Red Cross parcel deliveries had, in fact, fed the Japanese for four years, which seems a crime in itself. Nothing was ever done about it, and I often wonder how they ever got away with it.

One thing that was quite annoying in the internment camp was the fact that there was nowhere to get or buy clothes. I was just eight years old when we were first interned, but by the time that the war was ended, I was twelve. There was a lot of growth during those intervening years; some of the children were only six years old when we were interned and were, therefore, ten years old when we were released. It was difficult to keep up with clothing.

I had the 'encouragement' of having twin sisters who were older than me, although sometimes I didn't like it at all. They would pass down their clothes and I would have to wear out not one but two identical dresses; my mother always dressed the twins the same. So, I had hand-downs that came fairly regularly, but some of the children were left with very tatty clothes.

I very often ended up wearing a dress that had been made from some curtains. These had been hanging in the hospital block where we lived. There were, fortunately, some very clever seamstresses in the camp who could turn their hands to dressmaking. They used anything from table-cloths and bedsheets to curtains – just to make something to cover you.

Another great problem, of course, was shoes; our feet naturally grew during the time we were in the camp. One solution was to cut the front top off the shoe and let your toes hang out, but for most of us, it was better to go barefoot. It was very difficult after the war to get used to wearing shoes again. Being barefoot has something to commend itself; it is very free and easy.

CHAPTER FOUR

Victory in Europe

THE 'RUMOUR MACHINE' WAS quite important during those years in the camp. There was very little reliable information as to what was going on in the war, as well as outside the camp generally.

The crystal radio set was assembled occasionally and news was obtained now and again, but rumours were rife. The enjoyment of some was to start a rumour in the morning and to see how it came back to them in the evening. We were so used to rumours that in the end we used to sing a little ditty, sung to the tune of *Bring Back My Bonnie to Me*. I remember the words, which went like this:

> *The Russians have landed in Norway,*
> *Rabaul is reported to be*
> *In the hands of our staunch US allies,*
> *But that sounds like rumour to me!*
> *The guards are all leaving on Wednesday*
> *And the weekend will see us all free*

> *But look in tomorrow at this time*
> *And there'll be many more rumours for tea!*

The end of the war in Europe, VE Day, came in May of 1945 and we had been in the camp a long time by then. We did get the news, through the crystal radio set, that the war in Europe had ceased. There was great rejoicing in the camp; at least that part of the war was over. We were still prisoners – the war in the Far East had not ceased – but at last there was something to celebrate.

In the middle of the internment camp there was a huge bronze bell, hung in a tower that was surrounded by a big wire fence. We had been warned that no one was ever to go near this bronze bell but when news of VE day came into the camp, a couple of lads decided they were going to celebrate properly. Under cover of darkness, they climbed the fence around the tower and rang the bell. It made a tremendous noise!

The bell was huge, and the whole area around the camp could hear this bell ringing. We all cheered, clapped our hands and laughed – we were so pleased – but what we didn't know was that the sound of this bell was an indication to the nearby garrison of Japanese soldiers that the internees were in rebellion and that immediate help was needed.

Within twenty minutes or so, huge numbers of extra Japanese soldiers rushed into the camp. It was dark, but we could hear them screaming and running around and, after a few minutes, with bayonets fixed to their rifles, they were turfing everyone out and having a midnight roll-call.

We stood still, absolutely petrified – there were so many soldiers and so many rifles; we thought that we were all going to be shot. We behaved ourselves and after they had taken a count and found that nobody was missing, they let us go back indoors. Obviously, there were repercussions. The commandant of the camp, who was a nasty individual, said that whoever had rung the bell must own up and would be dealt with. The lads owned up to the internees that they had done it but were cautioned not to own up to the Japanese because the internees thought the boys would be shot.

However, such food rations that we had, which were poor enough, were immediately cut in half as punishment for the whole camp because no one had owned up to the misdemeanour. After about a week or so, when the rations were further reduced and almost down to nil, the lads who had rung the bell decided, of their own volition, that they would own up so that other lives could be saved. They went and told the Japanese that they had rung the bell. Fortunately, the disciplining of the boys was left to the internal internee committee. After this, the food rations gradually crept back up. When the news of VE day was confirmed and the Japanese knew they were losing the war, conditions in the camp deteriorated, particularly in relation to food, and our rations remained less than they had been.

Although food rations were now so depleted, the thing that was pleasing to us was the time of year: it was springtime and the trees were coming into leaf, whilst the grass was growing. We had been instructed (by those who had the knowledge) about the different grasses and especially about those that we could pick and chew on and those that we could eat.

As the grasses were coming up, we knew that there was something that we could rely on whenever we were outdoors. We were also told which trees we could touch and what leaves we should pick that were edible. We discovered that some of them tasted incredibly good. I forget which particular trees they were, but it was a real source of encouragement to be able to pick leaves, as well as pluck up the various grasses.

We were also given another little tip: most of us had blankets on our beds and, in those days, the edges of the blankets were covered with satin. If, when we went to bed at night, we felt very hungry, we were told to suck or chew the satin edging. We were told that this would help to allay hunger and, funnily enough, it did. I don't know why this worked, but I do know that most of the blankets we had in camp had thoroughly chewed edges!

After receiving news of victory in Europe, we had a few weeks to wait for VJ day – Victory in the Far East – which eventually came in August 1945. The rumour machine had been rife. We had news that the war was going badly for the Japanese and so we waited, very impatiently, to hear of news regarding victory over them. I believe that the Japanese surrendered on 15 August, which was a Wednesday. We heard the Chinese, who were working in the fields close to the camp wall, singing and shouting and giving victory signs – but everything was up in the air. We asked the Japanese guards whether the war was over, but I don't think that they actually knew themselves at that stage.

ATTENTION ALLIED PRISONERS

Allied Prisoners of War and Civilian Internees, these are your orders and/or instructions in case there is a capitulation of the Japanese forces:

1. You are to remain in your camp area until you receive further instructions from this headquarters.

2. Law and order will be maintained in the camp area.

3. In case of a Japanese surrender there will be allied occupational forces sent into your camp to care for your needs and eventual evacuation to your homes. You must help by remaining in the area in which we now know you are located.

4. Camp leaders are charged with these responsibilities.

5. The end is near. Do not be disheartened. We are thinking of you. Plans are under way to assist you at the earliest possible moment.

(Signed) A. C. WEDEMEYER
Lieutenant General, U. S. A.
Commanding

NOTICE TO ALLIED PRISONERS OF WAR AND CIVILIAN INTERNEES

The Japanese Government has accepted the Allied peace terms set forth in the Potsdam Declaration. Final negotiations are being concluded.

An official representative is on his way for humanitarian purposes and liaison with this headquarters. He will be an initial, pre-Allied occupation representative in the interest of welfare needs and general conditions in the area or camp to which he is sent.

He will coordinate with the Red Cross and Japanese Military and Government, all plans to assure the security of the personnel concerned, to take emergency action to properly house, feed, clothe and furnish medical assistance to such personnel, and to assist in maintaining order in camps awaiting occupational forces.

He will not have authority to act for the Allied Forces in the rendering of any decisions, military, civil or otherwise. Until such time as allied occupational forces arrive to accept the surrender of Japanese military forces, those military forces are responsible for all such control and decisions in conformity with the terms of surrender and the dictates of the Supreme Allied Command.

(Signed) A. C. WEDEMEYER
Lieutenant General, U. S. A.
Commanding

Two of the leaflets dropped on Weihsien Camp, August 1945.

The Wednesday passed and the Thursday went by as usual. Then, on the Friday, we actually had some confirmation that the surrender had been signed. The first indication that anything was about to happen was the sound of a huge aircraft approaching in the skies. It was an American B24 bomber and it circled high above the camp, came a bit lower and eventually came very low across the top of the buildings. We later discovered that this was deliberate on the part of the crew of the bomber, waiting to see if they were going to be fired on. When the crew realised there was going to be no resistance, the aircraft circled the camp again and then the bomb doors in the undercarriage of the plane opened and seven parachutists emerged into the sky.

CHAPTER FIVE

Freedom on the Horizon

THE PARACHUTES WERE BEAUTIFUL and colourful, and from where we stood we could see that there were men on the end of each of them. They landed in fields of *gao liang* – a cross between millet and maize – which grows over six feet tall. Immediately, everybody in the camp rushed to the gates, while the Japanese just melted away. The gates were pulled open and we ran out into the fields of *gao liang*. All we could see were the parachutes as the men were hidden by the plants.

The first people to come across the men found them with their weapons drawn as they wondered what was happening. They soon realised that it was just the internees who had come to greet them.

The seven men were carried into the camp, shoulder high, and they asked to see the Japanese commandant who was in charge. The commandant looked absolutely terrified, white-faced and shaking, but he was treated civilly by the Americans who then took over the running of the camp.

One of the parachutists was of particular interest to us. His name was Captain Jimmy Moore and he had been educated at Chefoo School. When he had heard of the imminent mission to release the internees of our particular camp, he had volunteered to take charge. He, of course, was especially greeted by everybody.

The seven parachutists who had dropped from the plane all had emergency rations in their backpacks. One of the things which they all had was a packet of pea soup which needed boiling water added in order to make it drinkable. These packets of pea soup were handed over to the staff in the kitchens who dished it out for the evening meal. Believe it or not, about fifty percent of the camp were sick because of the strength and the goodness of that pea soup. The rations we had been on had been so meagre and so horrible that it took a while for us to get used to eating anything decent again.

The American soldiers took charge of the camp whilst the Japanese withdrew to their garrison. There had been committees set up during the four years of internment to help maintain the running of the camp, so we were told to continue doing the jobs we had been doing and to continue keeping order. Meanwhile, the Americans tried to arrange transport to get us out of the camp and back to civilisation. It took quite a few weeks before anything transpired, but in the end (I think it was around 12 September 1945) transport arrived to take us from the camp in Weihsien.

We were transported to the railway station, together with our meagre belongings, and boarded a train for Tsingtao, which was situated on the coast. From there we were to be repatriated, whenever ships became available.

Train to freedom, September 1945.
Far right: Harold Chalkley.

It was very strange coming to Tsingtao, which was a thriving Chinese port and had many facilities that we had long forgotten about. We were taken to a hotel that had been used during the war by the Japanese for their troops. It was the Edgewater Mansions and, to us, it was the most luxurious place we had ever seen – and also, most probably, the largest building we had ever seen. We were stationed there with the seven Americans who were responsible for us until transport arrived to take us farther down the coast.

It was incredibly difficult, however, to get used to the freedom. For four years we had grown used to being so careful about what we did. We had not been able, for instance, to go for a walk without permission and we were not allowed to stay up after dark, after curfew.

Edgewater Mansions, Tsingtao.

Those first few days in Tsingtao were quite extraordinary really. It was a lovely city and there was plenty to explore, but every time we thought about going for a walk, we wondered whom we ought to ask before we could go and whether we were, in fact, free to go. Also, if we were outside in the evening, it was quite strange to realise that we could stay there while it got dark.

Those who liked the 'roaming in the gloaming' scene could stay out until the sun had gone down and until it was completely dark – and nobody minded. We did eventually get used to it, but it was quite difficult at first.

In Tsingtao there had been a Christian presence for some time. There was a Christian church and, on the first

Sunday that we were there, those of us from Chefoo were all expected to attend church. I was with my mother and father, as well as my sisters and brother, and we sat together during the service.

There were, surprisingly to me, some Japanese people in the church. I could not understand why they had even been allowed to enter the building. Much to my embarrassment and, indeed, my astonishment, I saw my mother and father go up and greet them after the service had ended; they even embraced these Japanese people. At that stage of my life, I didn't share my parents' faith at all and, to be honest, I would rather the Japanese had been hung, drawn and quartered!

Needless to say, I would have nothing to do with them – neither would most of the children who were there. For us to be expected to accept these people after four years of cruelty was more than we could endure. But I shall never forget the fact that my parents managed to do so; they displayed their faith in a very real way.

We eventually travelled down the coast to Hong Kong. There was mass repatriation taking place. The journey was quite uneventful, but it was nice to be at sea, which was calm. As we arrived, however, we were greeted by other internees from Stanley Concentration Camp, which was situated in Hong Kong. We immediately realised that the internees from Stanley Camp had been treated much worse than we had – they looked like walking skeletons.

In Weihsien Camp there had been, during the course of the four years, about twenty-four deaths, but there had also been about twenty births, so the numbers had stayed fairly constant. In Stanley Camp, so many people had died – I think about half the number that went in never came out – but it was good to meet those who had survived and talk to them.

We were taken to a block of flats – in Argyle Street. It was not on the island of Hong Kong but in Kowloon, which is on the mainland, up towards the Kai Tac airport where the British had a lot of planes and RAF personnel.

It was the time we had in Hong Kong – from September to November – that we started to really enjoy our freedom. We got used to being allowed to do whatever we wanted to do. Everyone was given a certain amount of money (I'm not quite sure where it came from – maybe the Red Cross) and I was excited to go out with some friends. Although we didn't have a lot of money, we went into a jewellery shop where I bought a little brooch. It was a little Chinese junk (a Sampan) and I still have it to this day. I think it cost the equivalent of about 6d, but it was the first purchase I had ever made independently so it really meant something.

Those stationed in Hong Kong, especially the British forces, were always keen to greet other British internees. One day I sat with some friends on a wall in Argyle Street (I can still remember their names – Elizabeth, Beryl and Barbara) and we spoke to some air force men from the Kai Tac aerodrome. Unbeknown to us, a picture had been taken of us talking to these servicemen and we later discovered that it had been published on the front page of the *Daily Telegraph* in England. As our names were written with the photo, it was the first news that my parents' families had that we were still alive. They obviously treasured those papers and showed them to us when we got back to this country.

*Left to right: Beryl Welch, Ann Chalkley,
Barbara Harle and Elizabeth Martin.*

The servicemen in Hong Kong, who were not in combat but kept their planes in working order doing sorties over parts of China etc., had a number of Spitfires in the hangar at Kai Tac. One day I went down to the airport with one of the pilots (unfortunately, I cannot remember his name) who asked me if I would like to go up in a Spitfire. I was delighted. He wasn't meant to be taking me, but he managed to smuggle me into a hangar (an enormous building) and got me into a Spitfire. It may have been a two-seater, although most of them had only one seat, but there was a space behind the pilot where I crouched down while he got the plane out of the hangar and across to the runway.

We went up and circled around Hong Kong. It was such a beautiful sight – all the little islands that make up that territory – and it was such a lovely clear day, with wonderful sunshine. I had never seen anything as beautiful before and I really enjoyed that time. Although I never knew who the pilot was, I am ever so grateful to him. I have never been able to thank him for such a magnificent day. It was my first experience of flight and it was a really good one, absolutely breathtaking.

Eventually, the Americans who had been looking after us and taken us to Hong Kong handed us over to the British, who manged to get the whole of the Chefoo party on ships home. Quite a number of those from Chefoo were not British – they were American, French or Australian – so they went in different directions. Those of us who were British, however, were put aboard the HMS Arawa bound for England.

My father's one piece of luggage was a cabin trunk in which he had managed to preserve, throughout the internment, some personal photographs and letters, a miniature model of a Chinese house, a few other keepsakes and a quantity of jade to bring home to England. However, whilst the ship was being loaded, a malfunction of the lifting gear saw the cabin trunk fall into the water and disappear forever.

CHAPTER SIX

Life Back in England

WHILE WE HAD BEEN IN Hong Kong my friends and I, who had no memory at all of England, had been talking to the men in the British forces and asking them what England was like. They painted a picture of green fields and blue skies, lovely villages and nice roads with cafés and all sorts of things that we could look forward to, which we certainly did.

HMS "Arawa" – the ship that brought Vicky and her family back to England in 1945.

Imagine my disappointment therefore when, arriving in Southampton on 15 December 1945, it was drizzling and foggy. I had never felt so downcast and betrayed! I thought that this was what England was really going to be like and that the forces men had made up a story of green fields and blue skies just to cheer us up. Happily, I have since then experienced the green fields and blue skies and all the other things that we had so looked forward to seeing.

From Southampton docks, we boarded a train for London. I must admit that during the journey, my disappointment with England lifted a little as I saw the lovely countryside through which we passed. Coming into London's Victoria station, we were met by my father's sister, Trixie, who had come up from Eastbourne, where she lived.

There were many, many happy reunions on the platform at Victoria with children meeting their parents again; some of them had been apart for up to six years. I was so fortunate that I was with my parents all of the time.

From London, we travelled down to Hitchin where my father's brother, my Uncle Bernard, lived with Aunt Dorothy. They very kindly took the six of us in and we lived in their house in West Hill which was, fortunately, a lovely big, roomy house. We were very soon able to rent another house in Hitchin and, therefore, leave my uncle and his wife to their family.

The first thing that my father wanted to do once we were settled in Hitchin was to get me into school. There was a grammar school to which he took me in order to be interviewed by the headmistress (which I found quite daunting) and my father explained the interruption to my education, as such. I was given the choice by the headmistress of joining the girls of my own age (where I would be vastly behind) or going with the eight-year-olds and catching up. I think it's not hard to imagine that, as a twelve-year-old, I dreaded the thought of going back to be with the eight-year-olds, so I chose to go with the girls of my own age and to try to catch up.

It was good teaching at that school. I don't know how much catching up I actually did, but I did manage to stay with the twelve-year-olds and was quite at home there. One thing that I remember clearly from living in Hitchin was the first time I saw lawns with daisies growing through them. My father got a lawnmower out and mowed the lawn, at the same time cutting off the heads of all these daisies. I was so cross with him for decimating them. I don't know if there are any daisies in China (I don't remember seeing any) and I thought that my father was being a vandal. It took a lot of getting used to things that you might consider 'English' when I was so used to things being as they were in China.

CHAPTER SEVEN

Living in the Capital

AFTER A WHILE, MY FATHER was appointed as business manager at the China Inland Mission in London and he travelled up on the train each day from Hitchin. My Uncle Bernard, however, encouraged my father to get a mortgage and to buy a house in London, thereby cutting out all of the travelling. My father had always been anti mortgages, or any type of borrowing. He believed that we should only buy or have what we could afford. On this particular occasion, though, he chose to follow my uncle's advice and started looking for a house in London.

My father liked the area of North London known as Muswell Hill and he found a house there which he thought was suitable. It was very close to Alexander Palace which was then in the infancy of getting television out to the country.

We moved to the house in Muswell Hill and we certainly enjoyed living there. It was a very popular residential area and we had good neighbours. My parents were Congregationalists and there was a church within walking distance of the new house, so all seemed well.

The China Inland Mission (CIM) headquarters, Newington Green, Islington, London.

After just a few months, however, my father started to get quite ill. He became extremely depressed and, looking back, I can see that he had, in fact, a complete nervous breakdown. I would suggest that this was probably triggered by his having taken out the mortgage, which was really against his principles. He had also suffered, like we all had, during the years in the concentration camp and he was very, very thin, having often given up his rations so that we children could eat. He found it difficult to cope with our new way of life, finding it extremely depressing.

I was quite upset with my mother at this time. My mum was a bit like the 'Church Militant' (that seems the best way to describe her) in that she was very forthgoing and courageous. She didn't really think that my father needed medical attention. She believed that if we prayed, he would get better. I can't remember exactly how that episode was resolved but my father did get better in due course. Yet it was a very long process and I don't think that my mother's beliefs actually helped him at that point.

Living in London meant that I had to be sent to another school in order to complete my formal education. The nearest school that my parents approved of was in Hornsey and so I enrolled in the Hornsey High School. This was a fairly large school, which still had assembly every morning.

I made good friends there, some of whom I am still in touch with, but the education part was difficult. I loved English language and literature and did OK with those; also, not surprisingly, I was quite good in religious education; but the thing that I could not get my head around was mathematics – I was absolutely hopeless! Even to this day algebra is a complete mystery to me. I cannot understand why y+x=z and I don't think I ever will.

When I had taken my matriculation (now the equivalent of GCSEs) there didn't seem any point in me staying on at school. I didn't think I would obtain any of the higher degrees, so I left school and, because I was good at English, I started to develop a real interest in journalism. I thought I might consider journalism as a career since I enjoyed writing about events and occasions, as well as inventing stories.

My parents found a secretarial college in central London called 'Triangle' and it provided a special course in journalism, so I enrolled there. We were taught the basic secretarial skills – typing, shorthand, etc. – but I found the journalism course brilliant.

The Triangle college was in South Moulton Street, which is right in the very heart of London; it connects Oxford Street with Bond Street and is very close to Bond Street station and almost opposite Selfridge's. I had an aunt who lived in Potters Bar at the time and I used to spend time with her. She was in charge of the personnel at Selfridge's so when I was at the Triangle, I used to pop into the store and have lunch with my aunt. I formed a great attachment to Selfridge's – I thought it was a lovely store.

Aunt Winifred, Personnel Manager at Selfridges during the 1940s and 1950s.

I also became very fond of central London generally and I used to walk around the area during my lunch hours. I loved walking down Oxford Street and Regents Street, as well as sauntering along Piccadilly; it was all very colourful and vibrant. It was incredibly fascinating to me and I still retain a great affection for London as a city.

By the time I was attending the Triangle, the family had dispersed. My twin sisters were both away from home; the elder, Betty, had gone to train as a nurse in York Hill hospital in Glasgow, whilst the younger twin, Mary, attended the Froebel College in south London, where she was training to be a teacher. My brother, Donovan, who was the only one left at home, was working for a large engineering firm in Kings Cross.

When holidays came about, it was usual for my mother, father and me to go to Eastbourne and stay with my Aunt Trixie – we would go there for quite a long time in the summer. When I was about fifteen, I wanted to get a job and I managed to get one at the Burlington Hotel in Eastbourne – a huge place near the pier. I got a job as a waitress there. I was very much the kind of underdog since there was a head waiter as well as a waiter in charge of my section of the dining room.

Being the new girl, I was put in the most disliked area of the dining room, which was the farthest away from the kitchen. You had to walk through the whole length of this long dining room to reach the kitchen, whereas in most hotels the kitchens are usually placed near the middle of the dining room. At the Burlington, the kitchen was at one end, with all the tables stretched out before you. The waiter in our section would take the guests' orders and then I would be sent off to the kitchen with the chitty, which I gave to the cooks, before being sent back when it was time to collect the starters.

One day when I brought the down the main meals for the guests who had ordered them, the waiter was busy doing something else so I thought that I might as well put the food in front of the particular couple. The lady had ordered spaghetti bolognese and as I went round the table to the correct side in order to place it in front of her, I must have tipped the plate. The whole of this glutinous mass of spaghetti landed in her lap!

I felt awful. But the lady (bless her) grabbed the plate from my hand, scooped the spaghetti back onto it and said, "I thought I'd have to eat it before it got to that level," and she laughed. Although I was chastised a lot for that particular error, I was always so grateful to that lady that she actually made a joke of it and didn't get me sacked.

As much as I enjoyed our family holidays in Eastbourne, there came a particular point in time when I asked if I could go on holiday with people of my own age. My parents had heard about a Christian holiday centre called Hildenborough Hall, which was run by an evangelist and his wife, Tom and Jean Rees. The centre was in Kent and my parents arranged for me to go there one Easter.

I was thrilled to be there. It was a pretty setting in Sevenoaks, and Kent, being the 'Garden of England', was beautiful. It was a lovely house and full of young people. The sessions we were asked to attend, mainly in the lecture room in the mornings, were interesting; they were not always Bible studies but were frequently led by visiting speakers.

In the evening, after supper, we would all go into the big lounge and there would be a more informal meeting. It was at one of those evening meetings that I heard Tom Rees speaking. As it was Easter, he described in very vivid words the suffering that Jesus went through. I had always thought that God had forsaken us in our early years when we had been in the concentration camp, thinking that we had suffered horribly and God didn't understand. Whilst listening to Tom Rees, I came to understand that God had suffered and that he understood what we had been through. It was at that point, after the evening meeting, that I knelt at my bedside and surrendered my life to Jesus Christ. I felt the most incredible sense of peace swamp me – a feeling of love and joy, and everything that was good. That was in April of 1949.

My attachment to Hildenborough Hall, with Tom and Jean Rees, grew very strong and eventually they offered me a position on the staff there, which I was very happy to accept. The pay was £2.10s per week, with board and lodgings all found.

During this time, Tom Rees was running a campaign entitled 'Get Right With God' and he was holding regular rallies at the Royal Albert Hall in London on a Saturday evening.

In the spring of 1950, Tom asked me if I would be willing to give my testimony at one of the rallies and I said I would – but standing up in such a huge venue, with about six thousand people listening to you, was absolutely daunting. With God's strength, however, I managed it. I then found out, on the Monday morning, that I had made the front page of *The Daily Sketch* – and with a photo included!

*Vicky (aged 16) speaking at the Tom Rees rally
in the Royal Albert Hall (1950).*

After leaving college and my work at Hildenborough Hall, the first secular job I had was with a small company called Karlit, which imported pegboard from Sweden. It had offices in High Holborn, in central London, an area of the city that was new to me. I found this part of London quite fascinating and I used to walk down to the department store Gamages, which was not as nice as Selfridges but it nevertheless entertained me in my lunch hours. There was also a very nice underpass that we often used, going down to Kingsway.

I stayed with Karlit for about a year, maybe eighteen months, and then I was offered a job with a company called Wyman's, which was a smaller version of WHSmith. They had offices in Bond Street and, looking back, I think the location was the thing that attracted me to the new job; I moved back into that part of London and stayed with Wyman's for approximately four years.

Travelling to Bond Street would probably have been quickest on the London Underground, but I found it terribly claustrophobic and disliked it. I chose, therefore, to take a much longer journey and travelled to work on three different buses. London transport has always amazed me as it seems that you get almost anywhere on a bus in London; so that was my preferred method of travel.

During this time, when we were living in Muswell Hill, there was (as I have mentioned before) a Congregational church that my parents attended, but after my conversion I decided to go to the local Baptist church. I found it a very lively church, with a large youth group led by a lovely minister called Ron Park, who had a very sound understanding of the young people's position in London.

A friend of mine in the youth group called Ruth told me that she had just rented a three-bedroomed flat near Highgate Woods and that she was looking for someone to share with her; she wondered if I might be interested. I told her immediately that I was keen.

This decision was partly due to the fact that I had an enormous circle of friends and we used to arrange what, in those days, we called 'squashes' – an informal evening of food and fun with an evangelical speaker. When I had asked Tom Rees to speak to a group meeting at my parents' house, sixty people turned up, which was hardly fair to my poor mother and father. So, I really felt that it was time that I left home and had a place of my own where I could do the entertaining.

For the first time, then, I left my parents' home and lived independently. I was, at that time, earning my own money – £7.10s a week – so I felt I was able to take on my share of the £5 weekly rent.

It seemed that at this time I managed to have quite a steady stream of boyfriends. There was a young man called Bob, who was from the same youth group – very intense and dedicated. Then there was Victor, who was with a group from Merrion Hall in Dublin – he and his friends were a very lively lot, they were great fun and it was good to be with them. After Victor there was Chris – he was different: red-headed, volatile and worked for Reuters news agency in London. Most evenings I was told what I would see in tomorrow's newspapers as headlines! There were also two chaps, Ron and Harry... but probably the less said about them the better, because I later found out that they were both married. Then there was a lovely young man called Bobby, who was a jeweller from Limerick in Ireland. But the best of all was a man called Paul, who was a pig farmer. I would have married Paul like a shot if he had asked me but, unfortunately, he never did.

After living with Ruth in the flat for some time, we decided to find a third person to share the flat and help with the rent. We found a girl called Kathleen, who moved in with us (we each had our own bedroom) and we got on very well, the three of us together. Kathleen didn't want to come to the Muswell Hill Baptist Church (where Ruth and I attended) as she had been brought up in the Brethren and she wanted to find a local Brethren Assembly. I didn't know of any local Assembly, but I said that I would make some enquiries and try to find out. Meanwhile, I continued to join in with all the activities at Muswell Hill Baptist Church.

There were a number of youth events that took place on a regular basis and on one occasion we were told that we could go to the Festival Hall on London's South Bank. This was in 1954, when the hall was quite new, having been built in 1951 to commemorate the Festival of Britain. We were going to hear the London Emmanuel Choir, so I applied for a ticket for the event, which was being held on a Saturday.

We went up to the Festival Hall by coach, if I remember rightly. I was very impressed with the venue, probably the most modern building I had ever been in. The acoustics were marvellous and the seating very comfortable. Ruth and I joined the party that was going to the Festival Hall; Kathleen decided not to accompany us. When we got to the Festival Hall, I sat down in the seat that had been allocated to me – it was near the end of a row – and a young man came and sat in the vacant seat next to mine. He started chatting to me and I soon discovered that he was with a group from Highgate. His name was Walter and he told me that he worshipped at a Brethren Assembly, so I was very pleased and felt this was a real answer to my prayers for a fellowship for Kathleen.

I instantly took the opportunity to ask Walter if I could give my flatmate his name and the address of his church. I also asked him if he would kindly look out for her, if she chose to attend his church, and if he could ensure that she would be made welcome. Walter told me where the church was, so I gave him the address of our flat as well as the girl's name. Having enjoyed the concert, we all went home.

Much to my surprise, on the following Sunday evening there was a knock on the door of the flat and when I opened it, Walter was standing there. He said that he had come to tell me that he had given Kathleen's name and address to one of the elders at his church. He went on to say that somebody would be contacting Kathleen. Naturally, I invited him in and we got talking.

Before he left, he asked me if I would like to go out with him the following evening for a meal. I declined (he looked a bit surprised) but I told him that it wasn't that I didn't want to go out with him; rather, that on Monday evenings we had our prayer meeting at Muswell Hill Baptist Church and I always went there. He suggested, therefore, that we went out on the Tuesday evening instead, to which I agreed. I found out years later that, despite being turned down for the Monday evening date, he secretly admired the fact that although I wanted to go out with him, I preferred to go to the prayer meeting instead.

On the Tuesday, Walter duly arrived at the flat. I was getting ready to go out with him and was looking round the room for a scarf that I wanted to wear; it was Chinese pink. He asked what I was looking for and he promptly found it, but wondered how I knew what Chinese pink was. I told him that I had been brought up in China so I knew very well what the colour was. Walter then informed me that he too had been born in China, in Shanghai in fact, and that his parents had been out there for quite a while.

This was a really good common link for us. Walter suggested that we ought to go for a Chinese meal, even though there were not as many Chinese restaurants in 1954. There were a few in the West End of London, so we went up to the Universal restaurant in Denmark Street, had a lovely meal and a very good time together.

After that first date at the Chinese restaurant, Walter and I kept seeing each other quite regularly, going out for picnics as well as doing various activities at the two churches that we belonged to. Romance blossomed and we got engaged (at Christmas time) and within five months we were married – on 2 April 1955 at Muswell Hill Baptist Church. Lots of my friends and family were there; it was a really great day.

When we discussed where we would like to go for our honeymoon, and having read in the newspapers that Prince Rainier had married Grace Kelly the year before and had spent their honeymoon at a hotel in Majorca called 'The Formentor', Walter decided that we would also go there. It was absolutely beautiful; I fell in love with Majorca, especially the northern part of the island. It was so good to be there.

Vicky and Walter's wedding day, 1955.

CHAPTER EIGHT

A Family of My Own

AT THE TIME THAT WE WERE married, in 1955, Walter already had his own building business. He was a qualified civil engineer but he was not particularly interested in building new houses, although he did build a few. What he loved – his passion – was finding big, old Edwardian or Victorian houses (and there are plenty of those in the London area) and converting them.

Some houses he would split vertically up the middle and make into a pair of affordable semis, whilst others he would split horizontally and make into flats. He was very interested in decent old buildings. The only downside (as far as I can remember) was that over the years, if there was a flat or a semi that did not sell quickly, we moved into it. We moved a lot of times – I think in my lifetime I have lived at thirty-one different addresses. In the end, I got used to moving and decided that it was, in fact, easier than spring-cleaning!

Walter had an aunt who was a florist. She had a shop in Winchmoor Hill, so Walter duly went to see her and asked her to do all the flowers for our wedding, which she kindly did. On the wedding day, Walter's aunt also gave us a gift of £5, which sounds paltry in today's economy but £5 at that time would have been a week's wages for many people.

Soon after we arrived back from our honeymoon, Walter took me down to Swanage in Dorset to meet some friends of his who lived there. Walter drove a Triumph Roadster, which was a sports car and the first one I ever remember going in. It was lovely to have the coupe roof back, driving down to Dorset. Whilst we were there, we were walking along the front at Swanage and came across a big antique shop (Walter loved to delve around antiques). Looking in the window, I noticed, right in the corner and leaning up against the plate glass, there was a walking stick. All I could see was that it had a white top, which I assumed was ivory, in the shape of a dog's head. Walter wanted to go inside and have a look around. As we did so, he picked up the walking stick and discovered it was priced at £5 – so we decided to spend his aunt's gift and bought it.

Later on, when I got back home and was talking to my parents, I showed them the stick we had bought and told them we had paid £5 for it. They were horrified. They thought it was an absolute waste of money and said that it would have fed the two of us for at least two weeks; they were not pleased with us at all. That stick, however, sparked an interest which developed into a collection, which then developed into a business. In actual fact, that stick was responsible for feeding the family for about the next fifty years – so it did turn out to be quite a good investment!

Walter was an only child and he made it quite clear that when we started a family he wanted more than one child. So, the next few years – the next seven years of my life, in fact – were taken up with producing five children. I seemed to be incredibly fertile.

We had a lot of fun with the kids and, when it came to naming them, both of us liked biblical names. We decided that any boys we had would have saints' names and any girls would have place names – so we ended up with our eldest, Sharon; then the three boys, Jonathan, Paul and Stephen; then the last girl we called Cherith.

The Meyer children.
Left to right: Jonathan, Paul, Cherith, Stephen and Sharon.

I'm not sure if any of them have liked or appreciated their names, but we always liked them. I did miscarry once, and that little girl would have been called Bethany.

Meanwhile, Walter often found himself visiting the building sites in the morning, setting everything up for the day and then, after lunchtime, having a bit of time to spare. He loved poking around second-hand and antique shops; his particular interest was in clocks. Walter loved old clocks; he loved the movements and the particular shapes, from little carriage clocks to mantle clocks and right up to long case clocks. He gradually built up quite a collection; he would buy very well and bring these clocks home. It did, however, get slightly excessive and we ended up with two hundred and fifty clocks in the house!

I'm afraid I got upset then, as you just couldn't move for clocks and we had small children. We had a particular falling out when our youngest, Cherith, was investigating the latest purchase (which was a movement of a clock by Thomas Tompion, one of the best-known clockmakers at the time) and she managed to pull the hands off it. This was not greeted very well by her father so we decided it was time that he had his own shop. Walter found premises in East Barnet Road in New Barnet and opened a shop, calling it 'The Dyal', which was the name of a famous clock shop in years gone by. So it was that a hobby became a business.

When our first child was on the way, Walter was eager that I should learn to drive. He didn't want to teach me himself so I had lessons from the British School of Motoring (BSM), and Walter was very keen to get me a car of my own. He drove the Triumph Roadster (a lovely car, but rather big) and he managed to get me an Austin 7, which was honestly like a little box on wheels.

On one eventful occasion, before Sharon was born, I was driving this Austin 7 down a hill in New Barnet and one of the wheels came off. There was a crocodile of little children walking on the pavement down this particular hill and the wheel from my car ploughed in amongst them. I was absolutely terrified that I had hurt, or even killed, one of these children. Fortunately, none of them was hurt. I was completely shaken up but I couldn't contact Walter. I managed, however, to get in touch with the foreman of the site where Walter was working. The foreman was a lovely chap, who came over, got me home and would not leave until my husband arrived; he actually sat on the doorstep of the flat until Walter appeared! Many cars followed, but I have always had a particular affection for the Austin 7.

The children grew up, taking up all of our time – my time, in particular. Having the five children fairly close together meant that the first seven or eight years of my marriage was a blur of babies, nappies, being pregnant and simply coping as best we could. The children, however, all had their distinct personalities and it was great watching them develop.

Sharon, the eldest, was a beautiful and a very happy baby, strong-willed and feisty. She suffered badly when she contracted scarlet fever at a young age, which took resilience to bounce back from. Jonathan was a good-looking child, but he certainly didn't enjoy the first six months of his life – he just cried and cried, all the time. Nevertheless, Jonathan grew to be strong and athletic; he was the child who was good at sport. Paul, the third of our children, entered this world at 10lb 2oz. He was extremely intelligent, quick-witted and absolutely charming, while the next to arrive, Stephen, was a delightful, happy, contented baby, though incredibly lazy. He didn't walk until he was over two years old, but he had a good sociable disposition and he was a loving child. Then there was Cherith; she was the last of the five and by far the easiest. Mind you, having had five children and Cherith being the last, I was by now probably getting to be a better mother. Cherith was beautiful and talented, and I never once heard her say, "Mummy, I'm bored."

Having the children all close together meant that if one child got one of the childhood diseases, the other four would get it too. One year I called the doctor on Christmas Eve because one of them had come out with big spots – I think it was measles. We then had to get the whole five of them through that. This happened with different diseases – whooping cough, mumps and rubella – and the last child was cleared of the last of that bout of infections on my birthday the following year, on 8 June. So, from Christmas to June, the whole six months was taken up with illness, but we did get rid of each disease in one fell swoop and generally had a very healthy family.

When you have a big family, holidays can often be a challenge. To help with this we had a VW campervan, long before they became trendy. When there were just the first two children, Sharon and Jonathan, we went back to Majorca and stayed at Paguera, which Sharon and Jonathan absolutely loved – especially the beach and the water. As the family grew, however, the holidays became more and more expensive.

After a while we realised that the cheapest option was to go to a Butlin's holiday camp. Once you were there, all the entertainment, the funfair and everything else was free. The cost included all meals, so there was little extra to pay for while we were there. The first time we went, we stayed at the Butlin's camp in Bognor Regis. Sir Billy Butlin certainly had his head screwed on the right way. He provided a wonderful family holiday, with all sorts of entertainment as well as competitions that you could enter – the beautiful baby, Mr Mod for teenagers, happy families etc. – and every winner of any competition got a prize of some description. Included in the prize was a free week's holiday for the following year. Our children often entered the competitions and won for themselves these free week's holidays. The last time we went, all five children had a free place and we only had to pay for the adults.

At the time when schooling became an issue, we were living at Woodside Park in North London. Close to Woodside Park station there was a very nice private school which was well thought of – a small school with a decidedly Christian ethos. We decided that, as the fees there were reasonable, we would pay for private education in the primary stage. It was a lot to take on, since there were five children, but we were glad that we did it.

By the time the eldest child approached secondary school age, we moved to Barnet. We knew that we would not be able to carry on paying fees for their secondary education. However, we were fortunate that where we lived, there was the Queen Elizabeth's School for Boys and the Queen Elizabeth's School for Girls – both good schools and highly recommended. The children were all enrolled in these two schools. They were happy, did well and made good friends. However, unbeknown to us at the time, there were drug dealers operating in the locality. They would hang around waiting for children at the end of the school day.

Unfortunately, Paul and Stephen were susceptible. I think Stephen was the first one to get onto cannabis but Paul followed, keeping it well hidden from Walter and me. I think their siblings knew what they were up to, but they shielded them from us.

The Meyer family.
Jonathan, Sharon, Vicky with Cherith,
Walter, Stephen and Paul.

Once Cherith was at school, I took more of an interest in the antiques business. Walter already had his shop in Barnet and so, in 1968, I acquired a stall at an antiques emporium in Hampstead.

The children used to love to come to the emporium – they loved the atmosphere – and, in their own way, they were also interested in the antiques. I started off in that emporium, but very soon I decided to go farther into London and, for many years, did three London markets every week. The first London market where I had a stall was in Camden passage in Islington.

CHAPTER NINE

Portobello Road

FROM ISLINGTON, I WENT TO the Bermondsey market in the East End, before moving on to the last London market in which I had a stall; this was in Portobello Road, which was definitely my favourite. It was such an interesting place to be, with so many interesting customers. The children used to fight for the opportunity to come along with me on a Saturday – I couldn't take all five of them together, so they had to take it in turns, two at a time.

My stall now had an eclectic mix of clocks, watches, porcelain and walking sticks – the latter eventually becoming the main items. Most customers already knew about swordsticks and those containing a whisky flask, but many became fascinated with those sticks that had a dog's head with an opening mouth which could hold a pair of gloves, those with a concealed ruler for measuring the height of a horse, an officer's cane containing a knife and fork, a publican's stick with a metal cup to measure a single or double shot of spirits, and so on.

Stephen, in particular, loved Portobello Road. If you have ever been there, you will know that the top end of Portobello comprises antiques and vintage items, whereas if you go down the road, it becomes more jeans and T-shirts. Right at the bottom of the road it becomes, more or less, junk – more like a second-hand boot fair. Stephen used to wander right down to the bottom of the road. On one occasion, he went down to the junk end of the street and found two Rolls Royce hub caps, which he purchased for his 50p (he had 50p as his pocket money each week). He then brought them up to the top end of the road, to where the antiques were sold, and he managed to sell them for £2.50. This gave me an indication that he would do quite well (which he did) working in the markets. Stephen had a very good eye and made himself quite a lot of money.

Stalling out in Portobello Road, London.

CHAPTER TEN

The Drugs Trap

IN THE ANTIQUE WORLD, there are people who we used to call 'runners'. The 'runners' didn't have a stall or shop of their own, but they were interested in the antiques. If you had something in your shop or on your stall which they felt they had a buyer for somewhere, you would let them run with the article. Stephen and Paul both did this very successfully.

On one occasion they were in an emporium in Bond Street and both agreed to run an item for different people. They went out and tried to sell whatever they had been given. Unfortunately, however, it somehow got out to the people in Bond Street that Paul and Stephen both dabbled in drugs. One lady had let Paul have something from her stall, but then began to worry and called the police, saying that Paul had stolen the item from her; this was totally false, as she had actually given the item to Paul quite willingly for him to sell. However, on other occasions both boys had stolen in order to feed their habits and a chain of events had started in which both boys were picked up by the police, taken into custody and charged.

That was a particularly rough time. Paul appeared in court and was sent to Brixton on remand while he awaited trial. Stephen also appeared in court and he was sent to Wormwood Scrubs. It was incredibly difficult for Walter and me. We had strong connections with our church – Walter was an elder there – and here we were with two of our children in prison. On quite a number of occasions, I drove into London to visit Stephen at Wormwood Scrubs and then travelled across to Brixton in order to visit Paul. They behaved themselves in prison, they didn't get into any trouble, which put them in quite good stead.

Before all of this happened, Paul realised he was too dependent on drugs and had applied for a place at Yeldall Manor, a Christian rehabilitation centre near Reading. Stephen hadn't applied anywhere. So, when their cases came up in court, they were both given suspended sentences on the condition that they went to a rehab centre. Since Paul had already applied to go to Yeldall Manor, he was allowed to go there. Stephen, however, hadn't made any arrangements so the court decided he would go to Bethlem Royal in Beckenham.

Having had them both on remand in different prisons, Paul and Stephen were now in separate rehab centres. The rehab centres had a strict policy that for the first month, any new inmate was not allowed visitors, letters or any contact with their previous life. Paul managed, somehow, to write letters to let us know that he was getting on OK and for us not to worry. We didn't hear from Stephen. That month seemed a very long time.

Eventually, the two boys came out of the rehab centres, clean and no longer dependent on drugs. They went back to dealing with antiques. Paul enrolled in a college in Hackney, where they had a course on horology, because he had picked up (from his dad) a love of clocks and he wanted to know about them, how to make them and how to maintain them. Stephen didn't have that particular interest, but did have a much broader interest in all sorts of antiques.

Paul stayed clean for years but, unfortunately, Stephen kept relapsing onto drugs and alcohol, both of which exacerbated mental health issues. He attended Albany Lodge – a psychiatric and rehab centre in St Alban's – many times over the next twenty years or so.

One weekend, just before Christmas 2007, Jonathan and I noticed that Stephen hadn't appeared at the Portobello market, so we went to his flat. Since I was unable to climb stairs by this time, Jonathan went in to look for his brother, whom he found collapsed in his armchair. Although we called an ambulance, Stephen was pronounced dead at the flat – he was forty-five years old.

At this time, Paul was living in Bournemouth with Donna, his partner of twenty years. Stephen's death hit him hard, as did the financial recession. Donna was a great support to Paul but, unbeknown to us, Paul had gradually slipped back onto drugs. In 2012, his behaviour became so erratic that Donna eventually had to move out. Nevertheless, she called round each morning to see if Paul was OK.

One morning, however, in late June, Donna found Paul unconscious in his bed. She managed to call for an ambulance but Paul was pronounced dead at the scene. He was fifty-one years old.

CHAPTER ELEVEN

Empty Nest Syndrome

INEVITABLY, HAVING HAD FIVE children in seven years, we ended up at one stage with five teenagers in the house, all at the same time. I remember that was a very interesting year – we never knew what was going to happen next! But it didn't last forever; as they grew and qualified in various trades and skills, they began to leave home.

It was fascinating to watch 'my five' grow up and mature. Sharon grew from being a beautiful child into a very resourceful, good-looking and capable woman. She worked briefly as a personal assistant to an eminent antiques dealer before settling for a career in nursing. Sharon married an estate agent called Richard; they gave me two delightful grandchildren, Natasha and Rupert. Following her divorce, Sharon came to live in Yorkshire.

Jonathan, meanwhile, continued to be the sporty one, often representing his county in athletics and rugby. He also qualified as a design and technology teacher, met his future wife, Helen, (also a teacher) and produced two more lovely grandchildren, Rachael and Philip. Jonathan and Helen also divorced, and Jonathan now lives in Norfolk with his new partner, Beckie.

Paul grew to be tall, blonde and handsome as well as being clever. He did well at school and went on to prove himself a brilliant asset in the computer world. Having fallen prey to drugs, he managed to emerge from rehab, go on to marry his wife, Fiona, and live in Hamilton Road in St Albans where he held stunning Bonfire Night parties! He also became a successful antiques dealer, specialising in walking sticks. Paul's marriage ended in divorce. He later teamed up with Donna and lived with her for many years in Poole in Dorset but, sadly, things were to go wrong.

Stephen was a charming, cheeky lad who turned into a popular, good-looking man. He was taken under the wing of Sharon's husband, Richard, and trained as an estate agent. He met Kerry, bought a house in Hatfield and seemed settled until the drugs and alcohol gradually got the better of him.

And, finally, there is Cherith, the youngest of 'my five' and my baby. She developed an accomplished artistic personality and enjoyed drawing, painting, playing musical instruments and has a beautiful singing voice. She qualified as an art therapist and teacher, married Andy (a civil engineer) and completed the line-up of wonderful grand-children by producing Oliver and Miles.

The empty nest syndrome, in the early 1980s, was quite difficult to cope with. We had a dog – the last in a long line of miniature dachshunds – but we did rattle in the Barnet house. It was a two-storey Victorian detached in a lovely setting, opposite a big spinney of trees and grassland. We loved the house and we loved the setting but, suddenly, when it was all empty, there didn't seem an awful lot of point to having it. So, after quite a bit of consideration, we decided it was time to move on.

CHAPTER TWELVE

From London to St. Albans

IT WAS DIFFICULT AT FIRST to know where to go. It was a bit like 'the world is your oyster'. We wondered about living abroad but decided against it. Sharon, our eldest, was living in St. Alban's and we often went to see her and the new grandchildren. We liked St. Alban's so we eventually found a house just south of the city in a village called Chiswell Green.

Although the first house we saw needed a lot doing to it, Walter was more than capable. So, we bought the house, renovated it, moved there and started to grow extremely fond of St. Alban's. It has a beautiful cathedral, a lovely park close to the cathedral, the Verulamium Park, and a good shopping centre as well as a market which is held twice a week.

We soon found a church, which we joined and in which we were received very well. After a while we were asked if we would become church counsellors. We were very happy to oblige, but we didn't feel that we knew an awful lot about counselling as such, though whilst in Barnet we had given particular support to one couple. They had recently joined the church there and we had been asked if we would take them under our wing. It turned out that this couple just happened to be Japanese and when I was told we were to look after Yoshi and Kaori, I baulked at the thought. I realised, some forty years on, this was God's way of dealing with my prejudice and all the hurts and feelings from my past experience.

Walter and I befriended the couple and they were lovely young people, completely open and sincere. Yoshi worked for a bank and Kaori was a teacher. We had the couple in our home so often that, I must admit, I gradually thawed with my thoughts towards Japanese people. I am still amazed at how God often organises things in our lives to bring about change – and always for the better (even if we cannot see it at the time).

You inevitably do counsel when you have a family, but we had never *studied* counselling or anything of that nature. We looked on the Internet, therefore, for places we could go to be instructed in counselling and we found that there was a Christian counselling centre run by the Crusade for World Revival (CWR) at Waverley Abbey House, down in Farnham, Surrey.

When we contacted them, we discovered that they did indeed have a beginners' counselling course, so we booked to go. We found the course extremely helpful and made many new friends at Waverley, especially Selwyn Hughes, who was the head of the organisation at that time – a very godly man, sensible and down-to-earth. He helped us a lot.

When we had finished the course, we went back to our daily life and to our work in the church. On our return, individuals or couples who needed to talk things through and seek advice would come to our home, sent to us by the church.

Sadly, Walter had heart disease, which he lived with for quite a while, having had heart attacks and undergoing triple bypass surgery in the mid 1980s. His heart eventually gave way and he died after a short spell in hospital in April of 1993. Sharon had been very supportive and would come with me to visit her dad. She was actually with me on the day he died.

Walter's funeral was a great time of rejoicing over his life, although it left me with an empty house and feeling somewhat lost. I just knew, however, that I simply had to get on with life as best I could.

For the next twenty years, I lived in St Alban's on my own, but with good church connections and close to family. I still had a car and could drive. Sharon and Jonathan both lived in St Alban's. Jonathan would take me to the market every Saturday – just the Portobello market. He liked the market himself, and we had great times together. Jonathan's daughter, my granddaughter, Rachael, used to come with us and I developed a strong bond with Rachael; she still comes to see me occasionally.

CHAPTER THIRTEEN

The Final Move to Thixendale

DURING THIS TIME, LIVING SOLO, I was having quite a few physical problems. I was suffering from arthritis and was in pain a lot of the time, but I knew that I could live with that. After a while, however, I started to have falls. My right leg, in particular, would give way and I would end up on the floor or on the grass in the garden. The worst time was when I became stranded lying in the rain, having fallen on my drive by the car.

Although I didn't like it, I had to come to realise that I had quite a disability and that I must learn to accept it. If, like me, you have been independent and active all of your life, it isn't easy to accept disability and it took me quite a while to realise that I couldn't go on much longer living on my own.

I had wondered about a care home and at one stage had planned to live with my oldest child, Sharon, in my existing home, making a granny annexe there. Eventually, having explored all possibilities and spending a few months with my son, Jonathan, and his partner, Beckie, in Norfolk, I came to live in Yorkshire with my youngest child, Cherith, her husband, Andy, and my two capable grandsons, Oliver and Miles.

When I arrived in Thixendale, I knew that there was a church in the village. I knew it was an Anglican church – St Mary's – and with my mobility issues it made sense to go there. I had never worshipped in an Anglican church before; my church of choice would have been a Baptist church, even though I married into the Brethren and had been used to a Brethren Assembly for thirty-eight years. Coming to an Anglican church in a small village, I did not know quite what to expect.

However, I was pleasantly surprised. The congregation there is not large, but the people who attended the church gave me a very warm welcome. I was included in everything that was done and invited to all sorts of activities. It has been a real eye-opener to me the way the Lord has altered my reservation and broken it down.

Firstly, I was able to join a prayer group once a fortnight. They met in another house in the village, which had steps that I could not manage. Sarah, one of the churchwardens who leads the group, suggested that they came to meet in my new granny annexe – that group has been going ever since and has proved to be an enormous encouragement and blessing. I am also asked regularly to lead the intercessions at the church.

Later, I was invited to join the PCC – and those meetings are also held in my annexe. From feeling completely useless and all at sea, I have been welcomed, given a job and a role to play.

I have found that one of the greatest advantages of being disabled is that I have time to pray. I have always had a quiet time every morning – reading the scriptures, praying and listening to the Lord – but there is a difference now. Since I have to sit in a chair all day (a very comfy chair, I might add), my mind is often free to think of situations and people – locally, nationally and even globally – and I do thank the Lord for giving me the opportunity to pray in this way.

I don't know what the future holds, I don't know how many years I have left, but I do know that whatever time is left, the Lord is with me; I know his presence is with me every day. I know that he is faithful and that he will take care of me, just as he has done over the many years since my birth in Hitchin, my early experiences in China and during all the challenges of family life.

The Meyer family as adults
(Cherith's wedding, 1992).

Afterword

I LOOK FORWARD TO THE DAY, whenever it comes, when I go to be with my Lord and Saviour. There I will join all the loved ones who have gone before me.

I believe we will have a really good party that day and I will dance and dance and dance. I will then go for a long walk with a non-arthritic, non-pain-wracked celestial body, singing my heart out to a faithful and loving God who has been with me and has guided and upheld me through a long, eventful and blessed life.

Meanwhile, the journey continues...

Postscript

SOME YEARS AGO, I WAS CONCERNED about my eyesight – things appeared a little blurred and not sharply defined any more. I consulted my GP who referred me to an eye specialist. I was then diagnosed with Dry Macular Degeneration. It was explained to me that I would not go completely blind but would lose my central vision. For a long time, I was still able to read and do crosswords etc. However, recently there has been a rapid deterioration in my vision and a consultant at York Hospital Eye Clinic informed me that I am now Severely Sight Impaired (SSI). I can no longer see to read and have felt depressed by the situation. However, my daughter has discovered that there are all sorts of aids available to help me overcome my situation. What I treasure the most is an audio recording of my daily reading notes 'Every Day with Jesus' by CWR which includes the reading of the scripture passages and comments. This audio version is produced by Torch Trust and it allows me to continue to start each day in the way I wish to. I have also benefited from products available from the RNIB such as my portable talking clock. Though new challenges arise, I know I can face them with the Lord's help; he never has, and he never will, let me down.

What Shall I Read Next?

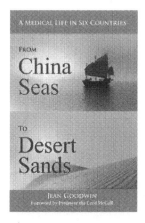

From China Seas to Desert Sands
Jean Goodwin
ISBN 978-1-907509-87-2

"...an exceptionally moving and fascinating account of a family of six who graciously adapted to working in five continents over seven decades.

Jean, aged 9, was captured in China by brutal Japanese soldiers and imprisoned with her family, where she was half-starved, lost much education, and her family life was totally disrupted. [She] overcame all these deprivations, and went on to a life of selfless devotion to others ..."

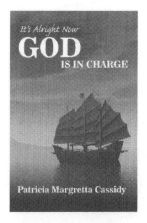

It's Alright Now, God is in Charge
Patrician Margretta Cassidy
ISBN 978-1-907509-84-1

The Second World War and the events that followed shaped Patricia's life as her family travelled from country to country and across three continents. From tigers and bandits to submarines and war camps, the stories of her family highlight the risks, dangers and sufferings experienced in Asia and Africa during that important historical period. Yet we also see how faith in Jesus can guide a family through every trial.